POWERED UP!

A STEM Approach to Energy Sources

NUCLEAR POWER PLANTS

Harnessing the Power of Nuclear Energy

CHRISTINE HONDERS

PowerKiDS press

New York

Published in 2018 by The Rosen Publishing Group, Inc.
29 East 21st Street, New York, NY 10010

First Edition

Editor: Melissa Raé Shofner
Book Design: Tanya Dellaccio

Photo Credits: Cover Phil Degginger/Getty Images; pp. 5, 7 (bottom) Daniel Prudek/Shutterstock.com; p. 7 (top) GraphicsRF/Shutterstock.com; p. 8 Peter Kovalev/TASS/Getty Images; p. 9 (Enrico Fermi) Keystone/Hulton Archive/Getty Images; p. 9 (Albert Einstein) Lucien Aigner/Hulton Archive/Getty Images; p. 10 colematt/iStock.com; p. 11 KENZO TRIBOUILLARD/AFP/Getty Images; p. 13 (Los Alamos) Joe Raedle/Getty Images Sport/Getty Images; p. 13 (Nagasaki bomb) Handout/Hulton Archive/Getty Images; p. 13 (Shippingport) https://commons.wikimedia.org/wiki/File:Shippingport_Reactor.jpg; p. 15 (top) https://commons.wikimedia.org/wiki/File:U.S.S._Nautilus.jpg; p. 15 (bottom) Bettmann/Getty Images; p. 17 Echo/Juice Images/Getty Images; p. 18 PHILIPPE LOPEZ/AFP/Getty Images; p. 19 (top) Igor Kostin/Sygma/Getty Images; p. 19 (bottom) ZUFAROV/AFP/Getty Images; p. 21 Monty Rakusen/Cultura//Getty Images; p. 22 HelloRF Zcool/Shutterstock.com.

Cataloging-in-Publication Data

Names: Honders, Christine.
Title: Nuclear power plants: harnessing the power of nuclear energy / Christine Honders.
Description: New York : PowerKids Press, 2018. | Series: Powered up! a STEM approach to energy sources | Includes index.
Identifiers: ISBN 9781538328538 (pbk.) | ISBN 9781508164265 (library bound) | ISBN 9781538328590 (6 pack)
Subjects: LCSH: Nuclear engineering–Juvenile literature. | Nuclear energy–Juvenile literature. | Nuclear power plants–Juvenile literature.
Classification: LCC TK9148.H66 2018 | DDC 621.48–dc23

Manufactured in China

CPSIA Compliance Information: Batch #BW18PK For Further Information contact Rosen Publishing, New York, New York at 1-800-237-9932

CONTENTS

An Alternative Source of Energy . . 4

Nuclear Energy 6

Splitting the Atom 8

How a Nuclear Power
Plant Works 10

Early Uses of Nuclear Energy . . . 12

Nuclear Energy Now 14

Radioactive Tracers 16

Is Nuclear Energy Safe? 18

Careers in Nuclear Science
and Technology 20

The Future of Nuclear Energy . . . 22

Glossary. 23

Index 24

Websites 24

AN ALTERNATIVE SOURCE OF ENERGY

About 80 percent of the world uses fossil fuels, such as oil, coal, and natural gas, as a main source of energy. Fossil fuels are made from the remains of plants and animals that died millions of years ago. Burning fossil fuels creates air pollution and causes Earth's temperature to rise, which is harmful to all living things.

To keep this from happening, scientists have been looking into other, cleaner sources of energy. One of these **alternative** sources of energy is called nuclear energy.

SUPERCHARGED!

Common alternative energy sources include the sun and wind. Others include heat from the earth, which is called geothermal energy, and moving water, which is called hydropower.

THE UNITED STATES USES MORE NUCLEAR ENERGY THAN ANY OTHER COUNTRY. THE WHITE "SMOKE" COMING OUT OF THIS NUCLEAR POWER PLANT'S COOLING TOWERS ISN'T POLLUTION—IT'S ACTUALLY HARMLESS STEAM!

NUCLEAR ENERGY

Atoms are tiny **particles** that are the building blocks of all living things. The center of an atom is called the nucleus. Nuclear energy is what holds the nucleus together. When nuclear energy is **released**, it becomes radiation, or waves of energy.

Nuclear energy is released in two ways. Nuclear fusion happens when atoms combine to form larger atoms. This happens naturally in the sun and other stars. In nuclear fission, energy is released when atoms split, or break apart. Nuclear power plants use fission.

SUPERCHARGED!

Nuclear power plants use **uranium** atoms, which split when hit with particles called neutrons. When a neutron hits a uranium atom, the atom splits and releases more neutrons. These neutrons can then hit more uranium atoms, causing a **chain reaction**.

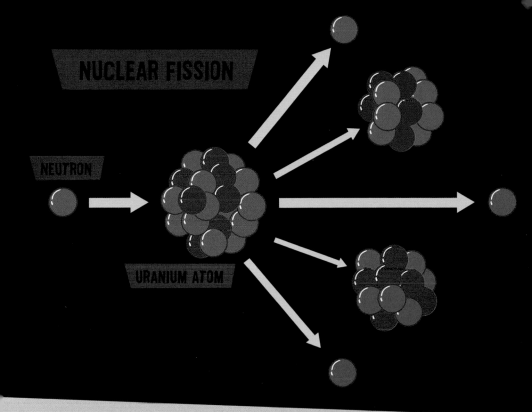

NUCLEAR FISSION

NEUTRON

URANIUM ATOM

NUCLEAR POWER PLANTS CONTROL THE FISSION REACTION TO MAKE A CERTAIN AMOUNT OF ENERGY. THE FISSION OF ONE POUND (0.45 KG) OF URANIUM PRODUCES THE SAME AMOUNT OF ENERGY AS BURNING 3,000 TONS (2,721.6 MT) OF COAL!

SPLITTING THE ATOM

Enrico Fermi was a physicist, or a scientist who studies matter, energy, force, and motion. In 1934, he split uranium atoms by hitting them over and over again with neutrons. He wondered if the nuclear reaction could be controlled to make energy.

Fermi invented the first nuclear **reactor**. He added control rods made of cadmium, a metal that takes in neutrons, to a nuclear reaction involving uranium. When these rods were added, the nuclear reaction slowed. When they were removed, it sped up.

NUCLEAR REACTOR

When Fermi split uranium atoms, the leftover matter was lighter than what he started with. Other scientists discovered that the missing matter was turned into energy. This proved Albert Einstein's theory, or idea, that matter can't be destroyed, but instead is turned into energy.

ENRICO FERMI

ALBERT EINSTEIN

ALBERT EINSTEIN WAS A FAMOUS SCIENTIST DURING THE EARLY 20TH CENTURY. HIS MOST IMPORTANT DISCOVERY WAS $E=MC^2$, WHICH EXPLAINED THAT A SMALL AMOUNT OF MATTER COULD CREATE A LARGE AMOUNT OF ENERGY. THIS WAS PROVEN BY NUCLEAR FISSION.

HOW A NUCLEAR POWER PLANT WORKS

Nuclear power plants don't work much differently than coal power plants. Both types of plants heat water to create steam, which turns **turbines** that produce electricity. The difference is the way the water is heated.

In a nuclear power plant, bundles, or groups, of uranium rods are placed underwater. Control rods are raised or lowered into the bundles to control the rate of reaction. The nuclear reaction heats the water, creating steam. The steam turns a turbine that powers a **generator**, which produces electricity.

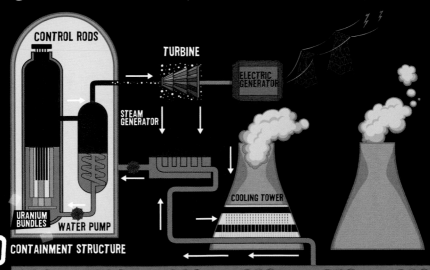

CONTROL RODS

TURBINE

ELECTRIC GENERATOR

STEAM GENERATOR

URANIUM BUNDLES

WATER PUMP

COOLING TOWER

CONTAINMENT STRUCTURE

INSIDE A NUCLEAR POWER PLANT, PIPES PUSH COLD FLUID CALLED COOLANT INTO THE REACTOR. A CONSTANT FLOW OF COOLANT KEEPS THE URANIUM FROM OVERHEATING AND IS VERY IMPORTANT FOR SAFETY.

SUPERCHARGED!

Nuclear power plants produce large amounts of **radioactive** waste, which may be deadly. The reactor is surrounded by thick steel to prevent leaks. It's also surrounded by a **concrete** building for extra protection, or safety.

EARLY USES OF NUCLEAR ENERGY

Most early studies of nuclear energy centered around weapons creation. In July 1945, the first nuclear bomb was tested in New Mexico. In August 1945, the United States dropped two nuclear bombs on Japan, killing tens of thousands of people instantly and ending World War II.

The effects of using nuclear weaponry were so terrifying that many countries promised to use nuclear energy only for peaceful purposes. In the 1950s, scientists began looking at ways to use nuclear energy to make electricity that would power homes across the country.

NEW MEXICO, 1945

JAPAN, 1945

100 METERS

SUPERCHARGED!

Uranium 235 (U-235) is the most important element in making nuclear power. Scientists can make natural uranium better by adding more U-235. To make fuel, the amount of U-235 is increased by 3 percent, while weapons-grade uranium contains over 90 percent U-235.

SHIPPINGPORT, PENNSYLVANIA

IN 1958, THE SHIPPINGPORT ATOMIC POWER STATION WAS OFFICIALLY OPENED IN PENNSYLVANIA AS PART OF PRESIDENT DWIGHT EISENHOWER'S ATOMS FOR PEACE PROGRAM. THE SHIPPINGPORT PLANT WAS THE WORLD'S FIRST NUCLEAR POWER PLANT TO GENERATE ELECTRICITY ON A COMMERCIAL, OR BUSINESS, LEVEL.

NUCLEAR ENERGY NOW

The largest use of nuclear energy today is for electricity. Nuclear power plants produce about 20 percent of the electricity in the United States. Nuclear power is also used in submarines, allowing them to travel faster and stay underwater longer. Nuclear power has also been used in ships that break up ice in the Arctic, space shuttles, and space probes.

Radioisotopes are radioactive atoms created as a result of a nuclear reaction. Scientists have found that radioisotopes are great tools in fields such as medicine and farming.

SUPERCHARGED!

Scientists are studying nuclear fusion—when atoms join together—to see if it can be used as an energy source. Nuclear fusion produces far less radioactive waste than fission so it's much safer. However, scientists still have to figure out how to control it so it produces enough energy to make it useful.

IN 1954, THE USS *NAUTILUS* BECAME THE U.S. NAVY'S FIRST NUCLEAR–POWERED SUBMARINE. WITHIN A FEW YEARS, IT BROKE EVERY KNOWN RECORD FOR UNDERWATER SPEED AND DISTANCE.

RADIOACTIVE TRACERS

Radioisotopes are sometimes used as tracers. This is because when attached, or stuck, to other things, they can "trace" what's happening inside those things. Doctors are able to put tracers in a person's body to help them figure out certain health problems.

Tracers may also be used to figure out how growing plants take in certain elements. This helps scientists create new types of plants in labs. Radioisotopes have also been used to keep meats and vegetables fresh by slowing the rate at which they rot.

SUPERCHARGED!

Nuclear **technology** can increase the world's food supply and keep food fresh longer, which means fewer people may go hungry.

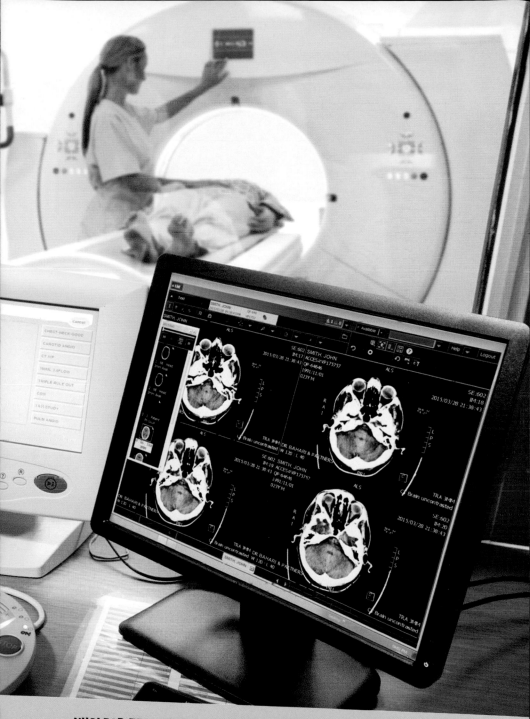

NUCLEAR TECHNOLOGY ALLOWS DOCTORS TO USE SPECIAL MACHINES TO SEE INSIDE A PERSON'S BODY WITHOUT CUTTING IT OPEN.

IS NUCLEAR ENERGY SAFE?

Radioactive elements in the **environment** can lead to terrible problems for people, plants, and animals. This has made people question the benefits of using nuclear energy.

In 1979, the reactor at a nuclear power plant in Three Mile Island, Pennsylvania, failed. The radiation released during this event endangered many people and the environment. This led to stronger safety rules, and fewer new nuclear power plants were built. Human error also caused a power plant in Chernobyl, Ukraine, to explode in 1986. This explosion created a radioactive cloud that poisoned people, crops, and livestock over several hundred miles.

CHERNOBYL, UKRAINE

SUPERCHARGED!

The United States creates about 2,200 tons (1,995.8 mt) of radioactive nuclear waste every year. Right now, this waste is stored in huge concrete bins around the country. Scientists are trying to figure out a better way to store this waste long term.

IN 2011, AN EARTHQUAKE AND A GIANT WAVE CALLED A TSUNAMI KNOCKED OUT THE ELECTRICITY AT THE FUKUSHIMA NUCLEAR POWER PLANT IN JAPAN. THE COOLING WATER THAT HELD THE CONTROL RODS BEGAN BOILING UNCONTROLLABLY, CAUSING FIRES AND EXPLOSIONS THAT SENT RADIOACTIVE ELEMENTS INTO THE ENVIRONMENT.

CAREERS IN NUCLEAR SCIENCE AND TECHNOLOGY

There are many professions, or jobs, for people interested in nuclear science. Nuclear engineers are scientists who use math and science to build and operate nuclear power plants. They also create new tools for their field.

Nuclear physicists are scientists who study atoms to learn how they can be used to improve our everyday lives. Medical physicists use special medical machines that use nuclear energy. They work closely with doctors to care for sick people.

SUPERCHARGED!

Today, many nuclear power plants have closed and fewer new plants are being built each year. One reason for this is the increased use of other, safer types of alternative energy, such as wind and solar power.

AS OF 2014, ABOUT ONE-THIRD OF NUCLEAR ENGINEERS IN THE UNITED STATES WORKED AT NUCLEAR POWER PLANTS. AT THAT TIME, THERE WERE 100 NUCLEAR POWER PLANTS IN THE UNITED STATES, OUT OF MORE THAN 430 PLANTS IN 31 COUNTRIES.

THE FUTURE OF NUCLEAR ENERGY

Nuclear engineers are working hard to create safer, less expensive power plants. The AP1000, one of the world's newest reactors, is easier to install—or put into place—and operate. It also has more protection against earthquakes and is less likely to lose electrical power.

Nuclear power could greatly cut down the amount of pollution in the air from fossil fuel power plants. Scientists are working hard to keep nuclear power as an option for a cleaner, safer planet.

COASTAL NUCLEAR POWER PLANT

GLOSSARY

alternative: Something that can be chosen instead of something else.

chain reaction: A string of events in which each one causes the next one.

concrete: A mix of water, stones, sand, and a special gray powder that becomes very hard and strong when it dries.

environment: The conditions that surround a living thing and affect the way it lives.

generator: A machine that uses movement to produce electricity.

particle: A small piece of matter.

radioactive: Giving off rays of light, heat, or energy.

reactor: The place where nuclear reactions are carried out.

release: To let go.

technology: A method that uses science to solve problems and the tools used to solve those problems.

turbine: An engine with blades that are caused to spin by pressure from water, steam, or air.

uranium: A heavy metallic element that gives off rays of energy.

INDEX

A

AP1000, 22
atoms, 6, 7, 8, 9,
    14, 20
Atoms for Peace
    program, 13

C

cadmium, 8
Chernobyl, 18, 19

E

Einstein, Albert, 9
Eisenhower,
    Dwight, 13
electricity, 10, 12, 13,
    14, 19
engineers, 20, 22

F

Fermi, Enrico, 8, 9
fission, 6, 7, 9, 14
fossil fuels, 4, 22
Fukushima Nuclear
    Power Plant, 19
fusion, 6, 14

J

Japan, 12, 13, 19

N

Nautilus, USS, 15
neutrons, 6, 7, 8
New Mexico, 12, 13
nucleus, 6

P

Pennsylvania, 13, 18
physicists, 8, 20
pollution, 4, 5, 22

R

radiation, 6, 18
radioisotopes, 14, 16

S

Shippingport, 13

T

Three Mile Island, 18
turbines, 10

U

Ukraine, 18, 19
United States, 5,
    14, 19
uranium, 6, 7, 8, 9,
    10, 11, 13

W

weapons, 12, 13

WEBSITES

Due to the changing nature of Internet links, PowerKids Press has
developed an online list of websites related to the subject of this book.
This site is updated regularly. Please use this link to access the list:
www.powerkidslinks.com/pu/nuc